The Characters Within

Befriending Your Deepest Emotions

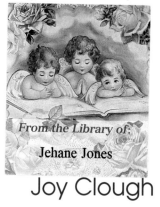

Joy Clough

ACTA

ASSISTING CHRISTIANS TO ACT

PUBLICATIONS

The Characters Within
Befriending Your Deepest Emotions
by Joy Clough

Joy Clough is a Sister of Mercy and currently serves as the Assistant to the President of Saint Xavier University. She enjoys travel, reading, gardening, playing tourist in her native Chicago, and exploring the great outdoors. *The Characters Within* is her first book for ACTA Publications.

Edited by Patrice Tuohy
Cover Design by Tom A. Wright
Typesetting by Garrison Publications

Published by ACTA Publications
Assisting Christians To Act
4848 N. Clark Street
Chicago, IL 60640
800-397-2282

Library of Congress Catalog number: 97-74028
ISBN: 0-87946-165-9
Printed in the United States of America
01 00 99 98 97 5 4 3 2 1 First Printing

Contents

Introduction

They came upon me in a rush, these Characters—knocking on the door of my consciousness, prodding me to put pen to paper. Wanting to tell their stories, some burst into words and images, virtually erupting onto the page. Others proved more reticent—making an appearance, inviting observation or conversation, shyly revealing some secret of their being.

They had a fondness for surprise—in several of their personal portraits, certainly, but, beyond that, in their very number and diversity. Such a crowd of them! Jostling. Wanting attention. Eager for recognition, impatient with such excuses as busyness or anxiety, intolerant of being forever judged and found suspect.

They first showed up on a weekend when I'd chosen to go on retreat. I had joined a group—strangers, for the most part—who were similarly seeking solitude, rest, renewal. Back in my room after our first session together, I listened in surprise as Simplicity whispered in my ear. Then Spirituality spoke up. Humor was there, and Hostility. Rage, Practicality, Shame, Wonder, Stress, Zest—they arrived, one after another in no particular order, apparently determined to dictate, sure I'd be their scribe. So I wrote. And kept writing.

When I stopped, I felt amazed, amused, enriched. I wondered whether these prose poems, these read-aloud portraits had meaning beyond me. At a sharing session during that weekend retreat, I introduced a Character or two to my companions. These Characters weren't strangers to them; my listeners recognized them yet found them freshly fascinating.

This book is a work of imagination. Yet, there's no point in denying that some dimensions of these Characters, that many of these Characters themselves, live within me. They live, I believe, within each of us.

When we meet them, they appeal or repulse. We find them clarifying and confusing; we judge them delightful or despicable; we suffer their tyranny and celebrate their tenderness. We invite them in or push them away. They shine or slink into the shadows, but seldom do they simply depart. Whether we humor them or resist, whether we welcome them or not, they hover and root. Befriended or belittled, they are *The Characters Within*.

With their delight in the unexpected and the subtle, with their determination to dictate words and images and associations, these Characters came upon me in a rush. Jesus advises us, "Freely have you received; freely give." This book, then, is a gift—to me and, I hope, to you.

May your reading of these pages be touched by the hesitancy of introduction and the warmth of familiarity. May your conversations with this company of Characters be graced by the surprise of recognition, the freedom of laughter, the wisdom of imagination, the relief of tears. And may your encounters with these Characters—and with any of their kin—yield insights that rise into words or settle comfortably into silence.

Acceptance

Acceptance is old now. Old beyond the counting of years, beyond worry over wrinkles. Old in the sense of timeless. Old in a category beyond measure. Wise. Insightful. Kind.

Grandmotherly in appearance, Acceptance seems frail but is remarkably firm of foot. She proceeds slowly but with purpose. Her gray eyes sparkle as they peer at the world through steel-rimmed spectacles. Her voice, her words, her certainty pour into your ear and your soul like music. And the elusive secret that Acceptance sings, the alluring words that whisper their way into your heart say not, "Accept your fate," but rather, "Know you are accepted."

When **Acceptance** whispers to me . . .

Anger

Anger and I are acquaintances—mere acquaintances. I find her rather scary—her long hair tousled around the chiseled features of her face; her hands always moving, opening and closing, beating the air as her words beat an issue; her voice sometimes strident, sometimes deathly quiet. And the company she keeps! Remorse. Bitterness. Sarcasm.

One day I began to notice other things about Anger. How she'd talk at length with Honesty. How Hurt would come out of Anger's office looking relieved. How, when she teamed up with Determination and Energy, the job—any job—got done.

My observations, however, didn't prepare me for a recent, more personal encounter. Anger burst into my office, breathing hard, frenzied, her wits definitely *not* about her. Hardly a presence to put one at ease.

Yet . . . I felt cleansed after she left, and there was something humorous about the whole experience.

And that's the surprising thing: sometimes Anger makes me laugh. An adult woman, she'll carry on about some petty thing that's driving her crazy. She'll rant and rail until even she has to chuckle at the absurd passion surging through her. So I'm wondering whether I've misjudged Anger. I'm thinking perhaps I should get to know her better. Maybe, just maybe, behind her wild-woman facade there's something— that touch of humor, the hint of hope, an edge of energy—that explains her apparent popularity.

If I got to know **Anger** better . . .

Anguish

There are no words adequate for Anguish—her twisted body confined to a wheelchair, her stuttering tongue loosed in wordless sobs of sound. It is painful to be with her, agonizing to feel the need, the hope, the despair flowing through her tight grasp of your hand. Her very struggle doubles back on her, tensing her muscles, tightening her tongue.

Anguish frightens me—her fierce distress threatening to encompass, overwhelm, drown all those who dare draw near. And yet, sometimes when I sit with her, I glimpse a quality of soul, a stripped-down shaft of spirit so lovely, so liquid that my mind twists and my tongue stutters.

I cannot convey it to her. She has no hint of this exquisite essence of her soul, of her spirit, of her being. It is the secret in my sitting with her; it is distillation and discovery: there are no words adequate for Anguish.

*Sitting with **Anguish**, I discover . . .*

Authenticity

Authenticity always knows what size will fit. What size pot will hold the pasta. What size lid will cover the container. What size shoes will caress the feet after summer's barefoot stretch.

And another thing. If you're trying to choose a gift for someone, Authenticity is a great consultant. Describe the person, and she'll tick off half a dozen possible and perfectly wonderful gifts. I've never been disappointed when I've followed her advice.

Interior decorating. Fashion accessories. The presentation of a meal. Authenticity has the knack—distinction with dash.

Did I mention that Authenticity never makes a scene about these things? She listens before she speaks, helps when she's asked, never takes offense if you make your own choices.

I could go on. And I did once. I asked Authenticity about her skill with sizes and gifts, colors and flavors.

"When I was young," she said, "my mother taught me to stitch my words and my deeds into a single pattern, and my father showed me how to hone my talents to my aspirations. After that, I guess it was just a lot of practicing."

Practicing, get it? Oh! I didn't tell you that Authenticity is a physician—and a yoga enthusiast—and a Catholic.

If I were consulting **Authenticity**, we'd practice . . .

꘠꙰꘠

Beauty

Beauty lives in a room with mirrored walls, an interior design she chose with enthusiasm but now finds increasingly oppressive. By day, for example, she notices how the sunshine and shade alter her image, how her reflection, multiplied, breaks at seams and corners. And there are nights, now, when she never lights a lamp amid the mirrors, when even a candle seems disturbingly bright.

Still, Beauty's decided to keep the mirrors. She intends to curtain some of them, gradually removing their veils until her original design is restored—its silvery splendor once again reflecting her from every angle. She'll not speculate about the time this process will require, but she's certain of her reasons. Once she wanted merely to gaze; now she's willing to see.

Beauty's *many-angled reflection reveals . . .*

Blame

Blame is a bony character who lives in a cave. He loves the dark dampness of his home, yet he's quite a traveler. Whenever Blame emerges into the light, the first thing you see is his outstretched, knobby finger pointing, pointing, pointing.

Blame speaks in a raspy voice, and though he's capable of a cruel shout, he prefers a persistent whisper. Hovering behind smiles and properly polite words, Blame seems to murmur "fault" . . . "your fault" . . . "should have" . . . "ought to." You never see his lips move, though. His message seems to come slinking toward you on the brittle beam of his shaded eyes.

Blame is brazen and insidious. He arrives without invitation, intending to stay forever. He lodges in the heart's crevices. He hardens the spirit's arteries.

Blame emerges when . . .

꧁꧂

Certitude

Certitude is quite a lady—regal in bearing, commanding in manner, accustomed to deference.

She was married to Meaning, you know, and they had a child named Detail. Certitude gravely assures all who will listen that she's had a hard life "explaining Meaning, attending to Detail." She repeats herself frequently on this point—the privilege of an old woman, I suppose.

These days, Certitude uses an elegant walking stick when she's out in public. She does seem stiff and a little shaky. Still, she's undaunted. She makes her appearance at every important event, and I've noticed that the younger crowd tends to hover about her, amused yet admiring.

On a walk with **Certitude**, I'd ask . . .

Counsel

You might think that Counsel is one to give advice, but that's seldom so. Advice is actually the least of things that Counsel is about.

Counsel is long on listening. She believes in the strength of those she listens to, and her faith is infectious. If ever you confide in her, you'll feel it. Counsel receives tears respectfully. She has a wonderful trust in the present, with its gathering of the past and it's opening into the future.

Often enough, Counsel will lace her listening with questions that probe but never blame or dishearten. She asks out of care, not curiosity—for your sake, not her own.

Counsel can shift the earth beneath your being with a gentle tease or a perceptive remark. "I should own stock in Kleenex," she'll say. Or, "No surprise there—gardening lets you play in the dirt while something's growing inside."

Usually, when you sit with Counsel, it will be just you two. But sometimes one of her close friends—Hope or Intuition or Affection—will wander in. You'll be surprised—or maybe not—at how comfortably they settle into the scene.

Counsel tells me she was one of seven spirited children. As an adult, she retains the grace of childhood, but she keeps her own . . . well . . . counsel. Her reserve, however, has ample room for hugs.

I think you'd like her.

Counsel *often asks me . . .*

Criticism

I used to be afraid of Criticism. She was so unpredictable, so moody. When she was feeling cordial, she could be stunningly wise, and on an average day, she'd easily offer a helpful insight or two. But if she was in a dour mood, feeling blue, angry about something, why, she'd shred you to ribbons.

Now, however, I know the code to Criticism's moods, and I'll share the secret with you. It's in her hairdos. If she's just shampooed and her hair is hanging in loose curls, get her to sit with you right away. If she's wearing barrettes to hold her hair behind her ears, you'll get a thoughtful hearing. If, on the other hand, her hair is up in a bun, you and whatever you try to talk about will go up in smoke.

Criticism, who really only wants to be helpful, is painfully aware of her wild mood swings, but I don't think she's conscious of her corresponding hairstyles. I'm not about to enlighten her.

While I think Criticism might be offended if I sent frequent gifts of shampoo, as often as it's seemly, I buy her barrettes.

Criticism *unleashed is like . . .*

Delight

Delight still scrapes the bowl and licks the spoon for the last bit of chocolate-chip cookie dough. She walks barefoot in the rain. When particularly pleased, she does a little jig. She loves colors and surprises.

Delight understands the fairy tales. Her own adolescence of seeking adulthood and approval strikes her now as akin to the poisoned apple, the wicked stepmother or the inaccessible tower. Delight's prince charming was Pain. Theirs was no happily-ever-after relationship; still, he taught her a new awareness of today. He gave her some fresh insights into herself.

Now Delight's concession to adulthood is an expanded repertoire of experiences. She can be six years old at the zoo; sixteen at a romantic movie; sixty at a card party. She'll gobble hot dogs at a baseball game or sip

brandy at an after-theater reception. She loves a
roller coaster ride and savors sunsets.

I've invited Delight to room with me. She's coming in
October.

I make room for **Delight** when . . .

Dependence

Dependence has had a hard life, primarily because of the nasty rumors that seem to precede her wherever she goes. People turn away when they see her coming. They've heard the scurrilous stories.

Pity, as is her way with outcasts, befriended Dependence. And when, after long acquaintance, Dependence invited Pity to her home, Pity discovered it was true what they say: Dependence does have a lover! Contrary to the rumors, however, it isn't Servility or Fear who shares hearth and heart with Dependence. No, her lover is Truth!

They've decided to run away together and start a new life in Kansas.

In truth, **Dependence** is . . .

Disdain

Disdain was an old man who wore a monocle and professed to know the meaning of perfection. His hair was silver; his shirts were silk; his topcoat, leather.

Disdain never observed; he measured. Seldom did he speak; he pronounced. He never lacked intelligence or income.

Disdain lived alone. Always. He couldn't imagine life—wouldn't have wanted his life—to be other than he found it—perfect.

He died of pneumonia.

*Through his monocle, **Disdain** never saw . . .*

Encouragement

Encouragement is a bartender. She likes working nights and is glad that Pretense prefers the days. She pours whiskey, beer, brandy, wine, even coffee— whatever the customers order. And beyond what they order, Encouragement knows what they want. So she mixes drinks and listens as the drinkers mix metaphors.

Encouragement nods a lot, slips in a word now and then, pushes the pretzels down to the guy whose tongue has come loose with tequila. "The thing is . . ." "What'm I gonna do . . ." "Listen, darlin'. . ." "I shoulda . . ." "Why didn't they . . ." "Hey, babe . . ." Encouragement has heard it all. She shines a glass, polishes an ego, prods her customers toward the door.

Patrons sometimes stagger out of the tavern when Encouragement's tending bar, but it's never because they've imbibed too much alcohol.

When **Encouragement** waits on me . . .

Exhaustion

Unwelcome, resisted, met with loud complaint, Exhaustion is no one's friend. How could it be otherwise? She's so demanding, so insistent, so unrelenting. She will not give way!

So it was that, whether I would or no, Exhaustion escorted me to rooms unknown. One was done in eggshell beige, its furnishings all china and crystal, antiques and collectibles. I didn't risk movement, hardly dared to breathe, felt brittle to my bones. An unweighed word, an unguarded gesture, and everything fragile—myself included—would shatter, littering the landscape with jagged scraps of loss.

Beyond the first, Exhaustion led me to another room, one of strikingly different decor. It was a scene done in dusty rose and cream, a space softened by sofas and mounds of cushions. Surrounded, embraced, something inside me gave way. I sank to my knees, my muscles loose, my breath a sigh, my heart awash in gratitude and insight.

Exhaustion in the guise of a friend? I only knew I'd crossed a threshold, and Exhaustion had held the door.

Exhaustion once led me . . .

Exhilaration

Exhilaration is a tightrope walker. He loves everything about his art—the spangles, the heft of the balancing pole, the poise, the way the crowd holds its breath while he balances overhead, the collective release when he quicksteps to the platform.

Although he grew up in the circus, Exhilaration isn't from a family of tightrope walkers. No, he chose that act because it matched his soul and sent his spirit soaring. The fear and achievement, the risk and success!

Oh, Exhilaration has had his spills. Life on the high wire, he admits with a knowing shake of his head, has its downs as well as its ups. As he's aged, Exhilaration has shortened his act, but he's never dulled its daring.

"Sure'n I know my routine by heart," he says—but it's heart, not routine, he bestows on each audience.

In my circus, **Exhilaration** . . .

Faith

Faith isn't gullible. He's well educated, curious, intelligent. Works hard—as a banker—and works out—as a bodybuilder. No one's more aware than Faith that those two are a strange combination. But that's how it is with Faith; he thrives on unusual combinations.

Like wearing two different colored socks on Fridays or outrageous ties on the eve of each holiday. Like letting his hearty laugh burst through the hush of the bank's coffee lounge. Like his remarkable and long-standing friendship with two old schoolmates, Question and Challenge.

At the bank, no one's solved the mystery of Faith's manner, but everyone knows he has an uncanny knack for assuring customers that their deposits are safe. At the health club, Faith is a favorite for another reason. Though it sometimes breaks their rhythm as it pierces their grunts and sighs, Faith's banter somehow lightens the weight members are determined to lift.

All in all, what strikes people about Faith is his ability to be both serious and silly. He enjoys, he treasures both these aspects of his personality. "Can't take life too seriously," he says; "it's much too precious for that." It's as if Faith knew some secret that the rest of us haven't quite grasped.

What strikes me about **Faith** *is . . .*

Fatigue

Fatigue always slouches. He sighs a lot, too, and never lifts his eyes. It's an effort to tell his story. Too much effort, actually.

No one understands why Patience telephones Fatigue everyday or why Surprise sends cards. And on Sundays, without fail, Encouragement shows up with helium balloons.

*Like **Fatigue**, I want visitors who . . .*

꧁꧂

Fragility

Fragility rings like crystal when adversity strikes. She quivers like a plucked guitar string. Quakes like an aspen leaf.

One day, Mystery whispered something in Fragility's ear, then lifted her chin, looked her in the eye, smiled reassuringly, and walked away whistling.

Fragility saw herself differently after that. Across her oval face swept the subtle strength of eggshells. She was crystal goblet . . . resonant guitar chord . . . towering aspen tree.

I think **Fragility** now knows . . .

Frenzy

Frenzy remembers seeing a squirrel racing wildly inside the garage once, and he knew it was an image of himself. He doesn't have many friends, but he spends a good deal of time with his cousin Fanatic. They have the same taste in clothes and hobbies— and girls, it turns out. For the prom, they're double-dating with Panic and Hysteria.

They'll have a riot!

If **Frenzy** sat still for a moment . . .

Gentleness

Gentleness has very small hands. She wears soft swishing skirts—so you always hear her coming, but somehow she arrives before you expect her.

Gentleness rides horses—bareback. She rescues kittens and finds homes for them. She runs barefoot in long grass. She loves flowers but never cuts one. Once she sent me a postcard from Georgia; the picture was of peaches.

Gentleness is a frequent and welcome guest, though she seldom stays long. When I let her use my kitchen, she whips up a soufflé or bakes popovers. Last time she was here, she left her lavender scarf hanging on a peg behind the door. I hope she'll come back soon to fetch it.

*When **Gentleness** arrives at my door . . .*

❧❀❧

Gratitude

When Gratitude was very young, her mother would often prompt her with the question, "What do you say?" And invariably, Gratitude would shout or whisper, "Wow!" Even now, in her adult eyes, there's a wonderful twinkle—part mischief, part surprise, part delight.

Gratitude has always worn her hair long. She favors the color turquoise. Her fingers are stubby and strong. She has a slight speech impediment and has never mastered the *th* sound.

As a girl, Gratitude loved crayons and finger paints, so no one was surprised when she grew up to be an artist. Her paintings and her pottery are precious— but not rare, since she's given pieces to so many people.

Now eighty-seven, Gratitude sometimes nods off, the hint of a smile on her lips as she rests in her time-worn rocker. She never minds being awakened, however, and the caress of her hand along your cheek is as compelling as ever.

Gratitude is everybody's favorite relative. Last week, she taught her youngest great-grandson to clap and say, "Wow!"

Gratitude's caress compels me to . . .

Grief

Grief leads a busy life—her hair pulled back in a ponytail, her sleeves rolled up above the elbows. She lives near the ocean, her house awash in tang of salt and scent of sawdust.

Grief, you see, refinishes furniture. Strips, sands, stains—sells her services to all comers without discrimination. Her own seaside rooms are rich in photographs and curios collected from a thousand adventures in loving and learning, in listening and letting go.

Sometimes of an evening, when Grief steps out on her veranda, she lets her soul go to sea. The angry waves crashing against rock rise up within her, or the murmuring tide swells and sways her spirit. She's lost then—tight throat, sore heart, salt-sprayed cheeks,

reels of memory wreaking havoc on time and purpose. Usually, it's Mundane, her housemate, who taps
into her trance, touches her on the shoulder and
asks, "Weren't we going to clean the kitchen cabinets
tonight?"

Grief smiles then. What an absurd question! What a
relief!

As I watch **Grief** strip, sand and stain . . .

Guts

Guts is the youngest in a very large family. His brothers and sisters, oldest to youngest, are Audacity, Intrepid, Tenacity, Valor, Fortitude, Courage, Bravery, Mettle, Daring, Bold, Nerve, Backbone, Stomach and Grit.

Well before Guts came along, the family had run out of beautiful names.

The beauty of **Guts** is . . .

Hate

Hate knows how to talk in sound bites, generate headlines and stage media events. He never believed there was such a thing as "bad press." Now, however, he's suing one of the tabloids. It ran a lurid little story under the caption "Look Again." It was a two-sentence shocker, and, imagine, the editors intend to claim truth as their defense!

Public interest in the case warrants this reprint:

Look Again
The Tattler *has learned that Hate lives in a house full of wizened apples. Whatever he touches shrivels.*

I visited **Hate's** house . . .

Holiness

I think Holiness owes much of his muscular build and his mindful ways to his work. For years he's been a garbage collector, and long before it was fashionable, he was into recycling.

Some folks regard Holiness with that disdain that's reserved for those who do dirty work. Others consider him a little odd, lacking ambition, a bit out of touch. His neighbors, however, find Holiness quite vigorous and friendly. He doesn't light candles or burn incense or whisper. He grows his own vegetables, enjoys a good poker game and likes to share conversation and coffee with visitors. He's a great conversationalist, actually—one who lets thoughts grow in silent spaces.

Once I spotted Holiness at a church bazaar. Like the rest of us, he was cleverly costumed for the occasion, but I recognized him immediately. His eyes simply can't be camouflaged.

Among the things **Holiness** has recycled
for me . . .

Hostility

Hostility seldom shows his face in polite society. Oh, he attends numerous business, political and social events, you understand, but he's discreet. You'll find him hovering over the buffet table or working the edges of the room—smiling, quick with a handshake, casual with conversational banter.

It wasn't until I invited Hostility to a party of my own that I glimpsed his true character. His banter covers blades of steel, and for hors d'oeuvres, he grinds the guests.

I recognize **Hostility** when . . .

Humility

I was never too interested in meeting Humility. I pictured her as small and mousy and uninteresting. So when I encountered her—plain spoken, humorous, skilled at drawing out others—well, I was fully engaged, enjoying her company before anyone thought to introduce us.

I guess I looked startled then. She laughed and winked at a friend. "Another one," she said, cocking her head in my direction. The conversation flowed on, drawing me in once again. It was a wonderful evening. Witty. Wise.

For me, an evening with **Humility** . . .

꧁꧂

Humor

Humor has a crazy striped bag in which she keeps a hundred costumes and a million tricks. She won't go anywhere without her bag, and you never know when she'll stop in her tracks to change outfits or pull out some foolish paraphernalia.

Humor loves a hearty laugh or a throaty chuckle, and she appreciates a silly grin. But, if the truth be told, her favorite sound in the whole world is a suppressed giggle—because, as you may know, it invariably swells into a guffaw.

Humor's well known in entertainment circles. And she's so versatile—travels with the circus, appears on TV, faces crowds to deliver monologues on a bare stage, loves the theater, publishes books of puns and other foolishness and stars in movies with box-office receipts that are no joke.

Still, Humor's more interested in people than in popularity, and she's ever on the prowl for an opening. She sidles up to parents in all sorts of situations and loves to help fathers tease young tears to smiles. She's a very popular teacher's aide. She frequently consults with doctors and psychiatrists, and is forever ringing up religious and civic leaders—usually when they least expect it.

Despite her incredible schedule and wide sphere of influence, Humor is the most private of persons. When she's alone, she dresses simply in white. And each month, when the moon is full, Humor sits outside all night, sipping white wine and letting her tears fall freely.

Humor *found an opening in my life . . .*

꙰

Innocence

Innocence was lost once. It was a life-changing experience.

It was night . . . a strange place . . . faces somehow frightening . . . people going about their business, ignoring Innocence. Panic seized her. Which way to turn? How to get home? Where to seek assistance? In an instant, terror twisted her bowels. Grief invaded her heart. Confusion seeped into her soul.

When she did take hold of herself and find her way home, she was changed. Hidden somehow. Hovering over something within.

Innocence rarely speaks of her experience. It gapes like a wound in her imagination. It pricks like a jagged nugget in her soul. Yesterday, she confided to me that she's now able to sit quietly, letting that nugget lie in her lap. "It's ugly," she told me, yet she knows she'll never cast it away. "But why do you sit with it?" I asked. She paused, then whispered, "There are hints of precious metal in it."

I love Innocence—in her secret sitting and in her public persona. Laughter and generosity, curiosity and aspiration, zest and affection all play through her still. But in her deep-blue, wide-eyed wonder there sits, now, a shadow of steely gray.

I'd like to tell **Innocence** . . .

꧁꧂

Integrity

Integrity knows that, by reputation, he's a "natural" wrestler. Hardly! There's been plenty of pain in the process of learning his sport.

It took long hours of practice with Courage and more than his share of bruises before Integrity could break the holds of certain opponents. (Embarrassment was one of those who'd frequently pinned him; Confrontation was another.) Grappling with Truth—an often unpleasant exercise full of sharp blows and surprising twists—helped Integrity discover how to win by yielding. (Yet, when he applied that lesson, yielding first to Denial, then to Excuse and finally to Pity, he lost all three matches.) Even now, having proved himself on a number of occasions, Integrity remains keenly aware that nothing can be taken for granted.

Courage and Truth approached Integrity recently with an idea: why not become a competitive team? They're skilled athletes now, experienced wrestlers, seasoned in their sport and respected for their personal specialties—tenacity, boldness, balance. They already have scars; maybe they could win some medals. Integrity likes the idea, but, as he pointed out to the other two, the only sure thing about any championship they might win is that another challenge will follow.

*Like **Integrity**, I've wrestled . . .*

Intelligence

Intelligence comes from a large—and annoying—
family. Smart, Knowledge, Education, Ability, Talent—
they're all full of jealousies and complaints. As if
blind to their general good fortune, these siblings are
forever bickering about who does or doesn't understand, who can and can't solve, correctly interpret,
decipher, analyze or otherwise comprehend the matter
at hand—as if life were an IQ test or an endless
competition for honors.

It's almost too much for their parents, Rational and
Intuition. They worry constantly about all their kids—
except for Wisdom who is not only insightful, like the
rest of the brood, but also content with life, a quality
that seems to elude the others. Beyond that, there's
nothing overtly remarkable about Wisdom. She was—
still is, of course—their middle child.

If I could get **Intelligence** and **Wisdom**
talking . . .

꧁꧂

Jealousy

When I met Jealousy, she was counting slights. She paused momentarily and invited me to join her. I did, and it was fun at first. But before long I realized that Jealousy's a miser, a fierce guardian of mementos and memories—ticket stubs and times when she wasn't invited, childhood toys and playmates' snickers, dried corsages and ranking second in any situation, photo albums and images of others' success.

Jealousy is proud of her collection, happy—in her way—to tout its worth. She cast aside as paltry my contributions and called my hard-won collection amateurish. None, she insisted, come near the scope of her estate.

Jealousy never noticed what I could clearly see: the coin of her realm, stacked before her, slanted precariously. Had the glaring light by which she counts and tallies blurred her vision? I could wrest no such admission from Jealousy. She wore her green eye shade like a badge of honor, and beneath it, the squint of earlier years had become a deep and permanent frown.

When I left Jealousy, she was counting slights. She noted my departure with loud complaint, and then, with satisfaction, added my desertion to her twisted store of treasures.

Leaving **Jealousy** behind . . .

Kindness

When Kindness was a child, he wasn't allowed to play in the mud. When he started school, his parents dressed him in knickers.

Kindness outgrew the knickers long before he outgrew his reputation as a sissy. Strange, how it took so long!

Kindness, after all, stands 6' 1". He wears a hard hat and works construction, driving foundation piles for skyscrapers. Oh, he did once salvage a bird's nest full of eggs that was found where a piling was supposed to go. And there was the time he got the union to okay a giveaway of three of his vacation days to a fellow worker who'd used up his vacation time tending a sick wife. Some people smiled; others shrugged. Kindness did things like that.

When Kindness went to his grammar school reunion ten years after graduation, everybody said he'd changed *a lot*—yet every single classmate recognized him immediately. They laughed about the knickers then, and at the end of dinner, Kindness ordered mud pie for dessert.

Years later, I recognized **Kindness** . . .

Leisure

Leisure *isn't* lazy, and, frankly, she hates being called that. It's just that she's devoted to pursuits that many people don't value.

Leisure is strong enough to sit still and supple enough to dance. She's insightful enough to savor others' poetry, and secure enough to try writing some of her own. Leisure has the courage to change, and she's woven that courage into the life roots that hold her steady—steady like a tree in whose branches birds nest and beneath whose boughs people seek shade.

Leisure likes string quartets and outrageous earrings. She wears her gym shoes without laces. She loves to play with children, and her most prized possession is an old tin tube of wooden Tinkertoys.

Leisure has a favorite aroma for each season: fresh rain in spring, lemons in summer, wood smoke in autumn, pine in winter. In February, though, when winter is weary, Leisure lights vanilla-scented candles. She sets them in the windows while she and Wonder practice yoga together.

Leisure would enjoy my pursuit of . . .

Maturity

Maturity used to go by her nickname, Mattie. That
was in the era when she kept lists of pairs: salt and
pepper, ice and snow, pleasure and pain—that sort of
thing. She's not sure why she started, but after a
while she thought maybe she could list her way into
the *Guinness Book of Records*. This and that, peas and
carrots, young and old.

When she wasn't listing pairs, Mattie was listing
appointments: shampoo and set. She thought maybe
someday she'd be a beautician. But after high school
her friends were going to college, so she did, too.
Fun and games.

In her English class, Mattie learned about plot:
beginning, middle, end. In anatomy, they taught the
bodily systems: skeletal, nervous, respiratory,

circulatory, excretory, reproductive. In social science, she studied governments: democracy, monarchy, oligarchy, theocracy. And in art, Mattie saw her first color wheel. Age and wisdom . . . oops, and grace.

At the end of her sophomore year, Mattie threw away her list of pairs. At commencement, to her parents' surprise and delight, she had her diploma inscribed with her full given name: Maturity Insight Gray. She graduated with honors.

Maturity graduated with honors in . . .

Melancholy

Melancholy favors rain-slick streets full of puddles and fragmented reflections. She likes to sit in window seats, knees to chin, lost in a stare, rapt in music. She prefers to sip her coffee in a booth for one, savoring some sweet sorrow.

Melancholy spends hours rummaging in wardrobes and old trunks, sorting fabric scraps and antique buttons. She's a seamstress who learned her trade by tailoring human dreams to mortal frames. She's seen, too often, the sad shock of customers whose fashion statements fell silent before the mirror of reality. These are the remnants on her shop floor that no broom gathers, no mop and pail wash away.

Sometimes Melancholy broods about all she's seen. More typically, however, she sits with the gates of her soul swung wide while untamed, unnamed spirits hover, successfully resisting capture, denying her the comfort of their confinement in thoughts or words.

Melancholy is similarly elusive. Almost everyone has met her; yet few have puzzled out the problems and the possibilities of the last four letters of her name.

When I think of the first two letters of
   Melancholy's name . . .

꧁ꕥ꧂

Mistrust

Once, years ago, I invited Mistrust to tea. I remember
the day distinctly. We had a grand time gossiping over
tea and pastries. But that night I was so sick, fight-
ing cramps, regretting the rich fare.

Now that I think of it, it was also about that time
that I began having recurrent bouts of insomnia.

Mistrust *affects me . . .*

Mystery

Mystery has very little to say. She's comfortable with just about anyone and only gets angry when someone mistakes her for her cousin, Problem. Lately, that's been happening a lot.

Like most of us, Mystery wants respect and acceptance. When she spends an evening with Silence, the air is full of secrets and awe.

I wish **Mystery** would say something
about . . .

Peace

Peace is a prospector. An old-timer now, he's never lost faith that the precious metal will be found.

As is the way with prospectors, Peace has simple needs. He loves a campfire. A plate of beans, a slab of bacon, a pot of coffee—these suffice under the stars.

It has never bothered Peace to work alone, absently humming, talking at times to his only companion, a burro. Lately, however, Peace has cast his lot with some other folks who love the simple life, work hard and know they'll someday strike the mother lode. It takes some getting used to, this being with others, but it sure makes for a friendlier campfire.

People I see living with **Peace** . . .

Penance

Penance comes from good stock and carries fine credentials, but most folks find him a bit eccentric. Admittedly, he has odd tastes. He buys clothes with scratchy labels and never cuts them out. He always talks to telemarketers. When it comes to vegetables, he prefers lima beans and brussels sprouts. He loves mystery novels but never reads the last chapter until he's put the book aside for twelve full days.

(Twelve, he says, is a mystical number. That may be. But I've dealt with Penance for twelve times twelve times twelve days now, and I've yet to even reach— let alone read —the last chapter of the mystery he is!)

What I understand about **Penance** . . .

Practicality

Practicality always wears an over-the-head, tie-around-the-middle apron.

She has a strong voice and uses it like a mother hen clucking at the chicks to keep things in order. She makes lists, orders wholesale when she can, clips coupons. She knows that Mondays are for laundry, Fridays for baking and Saturdays for cleaning.

I've never gone on vacation with Practicality, but when I was sick, she was a wonderful nurse. The broth was always hot, and she never neglected to smooth the sheets. Say what you will about her precise habits, a lot of us would be in a bad way if Practicality weren't such an industrious neighbor.

Having **Practicality** as a neighbor . . .

༄

Purity

Purity dresses in rich tones of gray to complement her deep-blue eyes. She lives each day deliberately— not stiffly, you understand—just directly and with heart.

Purity plays the flute and aspired to be a musician. In reality, though, she's a baker and her specialty is breads. Purity draws deep satisfaction from sifting flour, kneading dough, watching it rise, smelling it bake. She never gives Christmas gifts, but in the middle of March or on a hot day in August, you're liable to get a loaf of bread delivered to your door.

When Purity goes on a picnic, she carries an old wicker basket that belonged to her grandmother, and she covers its contents with a red-checked tablecloth that a dear friend gave her years ago. Whatever else may be in the basket, there will always be champagne.

I find that **Purity's** basket always has . . .

Rage

Rage is an old woman with swollen ankles and tight lips. She never says much, but you sense an explosion waiting to happen. In her presence, if you're not afraid, you're sad.

When **Rage** explodes . . .

Revenge

Revenge has terrible arthritis; he can't unclench his fists. For that reason, he never wears anything with buttons. Zippers are manageable, but Velcro is best— and besides, Revenge loves the ripping sound it makes.

Last week, Revenge cut his foot stomping down flowers that were blooming in his alley. The doctor is afraid he has lockjaw.

What I enjoy about **Revenge** . . .

Routine

Routine takes the 8:03 a.m. train to work every
weekday morning. She always carries her umbrella and
wears her gym shoes. She keeps her dress shoes in
the lower right-hand drawer of her desk at the office.

Routine catches the 5:27 p.m. train home. She reads
the newspaper, pages one through nine, and never
leaves her seat until the conductor calls her stop.

Routine isn't married. She never watches television
while she's eating. She always waters her plants on
Tuesdays. She wears navy blue on even numbered
days and burgundy or gray on the others.

Routine was shattered one day when her alarm clock
failed. She had to catch the 8:08 to work. It fright-
ened her to be so out of control, but then—without

precedent or explanation—she *decided* to take the 6:01 home.

Routine doesn't understand what got into her that day. When she remembers it, she shudders—but it was sort of exciting!

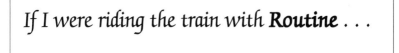

If I were riding the train with **Routine** . . .

Shame

Shame is a girl child who sits with her hands folded in her lap. It takes a lot of coaxing to get her to look at you, and then the glance is furtive. Her lips tremble sometimes, but she never cries or cries out.

Shame has a doll that she pinches when no one is looking. It makes her feel better; it makes her feel worse.

Shame is neat and clean, well dressed, polite, a model child. She's named for an aunt who committed suicide at age twenty-three.

Shame never cries because . . .

Silence

Silence lives in a simple house where what captures your attention is his sense of the artistic. The walls of each room have but one adornment.

In the living room: a red-framed photo, a landscape of undisturbed snow edged by trees. In the study: a crush of people on a busy street, people whose faces—despite myriad moods—capture the shared fragility of human life. In the kitchen: a triptych of his parents as children, as newlyweds, as grandparents. In the bedroom: a bold print of purple fireweed shot from a low angle, looking like soft spears piercing the heavens.

"They are enough," Silence says of his photographs and paintings. "They fill the house with harmony."

In **Silence's** house, I notice . . .

Simplicity

I wish I had the right words to introduce Simplicity. Limpid, rooted, chaste—words of that sort come to mind. Yet, she's more elusive, more attractive, more fulsome than any of those terms.

Simplicity is free of craving and full of contentment. Perhaps it would help to know that she collects seashells. Or that she eats her popcorn plain. Or that she has a flair for making gift wrap out of white tissue paper and brightly colored markers. Or that she keeps a quilt on her couch and wears old corduroy slippers.

I love to be with Simplicity. She always makes me feel comfortable, and she amazes me with visions of beauty beneath the mundane. This morning she dropped by bringing me a bouquet of dandelions, violets and clover. She'd just seen a butterfly.

Simplicity is elusive because . . .

Spirituality

Spirituality is more at ease with herself than she's ever been before. She distinctly remembers the day she began to change. She was in a strange city, using the telephone directory—the yellow pages—when she saw her name—*Spirituality*—listed under R for *Restaurants*. That was rather comical; everyone knew that the proper R listing was *Religion*.

But Spirituality's clever. She could see a connection—food, nourishment. "Feed the soul" was a pretty good variation on "Feed my sheep."

"Feed the soul." It haunted her, prompted her to go to the art museum, urged her to buy theater tickets, teased her into attending outdoor concerts, actually got her to call old friends for lunch.

Then, about this time last year, Spirituality fell into a cleaning frenzy. Cleaned out her closet: got rid of most of her business suits and bought a variety of wraparound skirts. Attacked the utility room: why so many half-worn sponge mops? Finally, the medicine chest: in with some bath oil; out with the mineral oil.

Last month, Spirituality realized that she was savoring the quiet of early morning. She found herself ending most days with a grateful prayer. And yesterday, when Duty stopped her on the street to admonish her for singing, Spirituality listened agreeably, and then went on her way. Unperturbed, undeterred and humming.

I, too, remember when **Spirituality** began
   to change . . .

꙳꙳꙳

Stress

Stress wrote a parody of "These Are a Few of My Favorite Things," and everyone who heard it wanted a copy. They seemed to find it quite singable, which worried Stress, but she was reassured when told that she might be sued for copyright infringement. In fact, that was the deciding factor: she rushed her parody into print.

In case you're interested, here it is:

Long nails on blackboards and lines that move slowly,
Rush-hour traffic, the demand to act holy,
Autos that won't start from autumn to spring—
Stress finds that these are just wonderful things.

Loud crabby bosses and kids who are whiny,
Credit that's questioned and print that is tiny,

Boom boxes blaring and street beggars' pleas—
Stress recommends you try pleasures like these.

Car alarms' screech,
  supper sales calls,
    bills that can't be paid—
Stress knows that you will enjoy these with her...
Her favorites, her stock in trade.

These days, Stress hears her song ad nauseam.
Everyone's singing it, and it's driving her crazy. She
couldn't be happier!

Lines I'd add to **Stress's** song . . .

Stubbornness

It's sad about Stubbornness and the way she's stuck in bed. It's not paralysis. She's put on so much weight, she simply can't move.

She can still give orders though. "Pout 'n' Shout" the neighbor children call her.

There's really very little hope for Stubbornness unless her daughter Timidity can find the nerve to stop feeding her everything she craves. Actually, late last night, Timidity did refuse to make a hot-fudge sundae for Stubbornness when she was screaming for one. They were both so surprised that Stubbornness fell silent and Timidity slid her tongue smoothly over some words without stammering.

Someone going by the house around midnight said he heard laughter, but he must have been mistaken. Stubbornness never laughs.

Stubbornness craves . . .

⚜

Stupidity

Stupidity and Foolishness are twins, but their differences are more striking than their similarities. Stupidity, for example, is often petulant, while Foolishness is lighthearted. Stupidity can be stubborn and is usually quite serious; Foolishness, as you might imagine, is more flexible and certainly more open to surprises.

Having grown up side by side, Stupidity and Foolishness gladly set out on separate adult lives. They never agreed on all manner of topics. Wardrobe, for instance. Stupidity favors suits and coordinated casuals; Foolishness is all colors and scarves. Having pursued the same major in college, and twins though they are, they chose curiously apt but divergent careers. Foolishness designs playgrounds; Stupidity is a stationary engineer.

But their differences run deeper than tastes or professions. Stupidity, you see, is extremely embarrassed by Foolishness's antics—though I've observed that Foolishness seems able to laugh at Stupidity's lapses. Personally, I find them both thoughtless and maddening at times. Even so, Foolishness will ask forgiveness, but Stupidity seldom sees need for an apology.

Most telling, however, was the funeral—the day I blurted out my intense loneliness at the loss of my own twin. "I know exactly how you feel," said Stupidity looking solemn. "Oh," murmured Foolishness, draping a scarf around my shoulders.

I kept the scarf. To tell the truth, on more than one occasion, it's been a comfort or eased a burden. And I never said thank you. Stupid of me.

The last time I ran into **Stupidity** . . .

Suspicion

Suspicion was always smooth. His confident air and his inside information—imparted with a knowing nod of the head—intrigued others and contributed mightily to his apparent popularity and evident success. But all that's changed since the accident.

You heard about the accident, surely? Suspicion was riding his ten-speed. After a fast run down a long hill, while looking over his shoulder to guard his rear, he hit a protective railing, flipped off and rocketed onto the road. Luckily, he was wearing a helmet.

Still, Suspicion's speech is slurred now, and he's lost vocal control; often, quite inadvertently, he shouts. He who loved parties has withdrawn from society. Even at home, he keeps the curtains drawn, his eyes ever darting toward the shadowy corners of his room.

He fidgets and whimpers, all his old polish and sophistication—gone.

Suspicion has second thoughts about his so-called friends and their notion that he should get back on a bike. And he's not sure what to make of his buddy Sarcasm's recent gift of a rearview mirror with handlebar mounting. Even before he opened the gift—just for an instant, mind you—he thought Sarcasm's familiar and ready smile seemed somehow like a sneer.

I suspect **Suspicion** . . .

Tedium

Last Christmas, I gave Tedium red-plaid boxer shorts. He pouted. He poked at them as if they'd burn or bite. He subdued them with the lid of the box.

Tedium tempts me toward such outrageous acts. He shuffles. He whines. His days run a cotton gauntlet of routine. Tedium never notices chance events—a goldfinch at the feeder, a penny on the sidewalk. Red-plaid boxer shorts caught the attention of this man who prefers gray.

Months later, Tedium confided that he actually wore them on April Fool's Day. I stared; I smiled; I laughed. What imagination! What daring! What next?

I'd like to give **Tedium** . . .

Vulnerability

Early each morning Vulnerability goes out to her garden to sit. Sometimes she sips coffee; sometimes she cries; sometimes she just sits—amazed later at the passage of time. Usually, she visits the flowers.

A few years ago, Vulnerability took up gardening; without quite realizing what was happening, she discovered the quiet, steady, sometimes tedious, sometimes surprising story of the soil. As if they were the only confidants she could trust, Vulnerability whispered her secrets to trees and murmured her insights to small creatures of the earth. Gradually, she felt free to lie on the lawn and consider clouds. Sometimes lately she's heard herself exclaiming encouragingly over whatever is rooting or blossoming, wriggling or buzzing by.

Some might call her a little odd, even slightly crazy, but Vulnerability's open to the risk. Just this morning she realized that for months Authenticity's been exclaiming encouragingly over her!

Vulnerability helped me discover . . .

Wonder

Wonder is five years old and almost always on tiptoe. His wide brown eyes peer into everything—the bug in the grass, the light in the refrigerator, the crack in your heart.

Wonder claps his excitement with dirty hands. He spills his laughter over delight, hushes awe across your lips and yells surprise into your soul.

Wonder's hair is always in his eyes. His shirt is never in his pants. His curiosity and his nose wiggle. Only the lure of licorice can keep him from leaping into a new adventure.

Did I say Wonder was five years old? Sorry, I meant fifty.

I wonder whether **Wonder** . . .

Zeal

Sometimes Zeal can't get his words out fast enough, he has so much to say. And he's not just a talker. Zeal's the first to roll up his sleeves to get a job done—and often the last to roll them down again.

Zeal loves to travel. He's been to India and Turkey, Kenya and Japan, Peru and Alaska. Mountains— mountains are Zeal's love, especially if they have waterfalls. He climbs and camps and—few people know this about him—contemplates.

One time, in Ireland, Zeal met a look-alike, a veritable twin named Zealot. They didn't get along at all.

I've seldom seen Zeal tired, but once I caught him lying under a tree watching clouds. And when I dine with him, I notice that he never seems rushed. No one can savor a single glass of good sherry as lovingly as Zeal.

Because of **Zeal**, I've . . .

Zest

Zest gets tired of always being last in lines arranged alphabetically. For a while, he thought of changing his name to Verve, but that really wouldn't have accomplished much. Someone suggested he could really get ahead if he went by the name Energy, but somehow it didn't appeal to him.

Zest is fascinated by motion. He's terrific on a skateboard and when rollerblades appeared, Zest was one of the first to master them. Yet, when he was laid up with a broken leg (a skiing accident), Zest discovered that motion isn't only physical. He sat in his wheelchair and plunged into a whole new world.

Tomorrow, Zest is setting out on a cross-country bicycle trip. Alone, but confident that he'll meet many fascinating people along the way. He knows that every community has its biking, skateboard or rollerblade enthusiasts. But he's particularly looking forward to chatting with people in wheelchairs.

Zest moves me . . .

Afterword

An author is forever revising, and my encounter with
these Characters has proved no exception to that rule.
Reading their revelations, listening to the language with
my inner ear, I more than once altered an image, found a
fresh word, expanded or condensed or reordered the
profile I was pondering for a second or third or suppos-
edly final time. Even as I worked on the text, however,
the Characters were working on me. An image that
seemed mysteriously apt when first employed would
suddenly open into new levels of meaning. An account
that seemed accurate at its writing would suddenly seem
flat and somehow off the mark. A description originally
beset with the difficulty of elusive words or contrived
images or forced feeling would suddenly appear fluid and
insightful. While several playful profiles continued to
prompt laughter, the ominous ones suddenly proved
particularly powerful, even compelling. And with each
rereading, these impressions altered yet again. Would I
never finish?

In the essential sense, no. That was the lesson of edit-
ing—the Characters were teaching me anew that they are
indeed dynamic. And complex. And mischievous. They

simply will not be captured or fixed upon a page. They love to surprise with unexpected evidence of growth or change, with subtle shifts of emphasis or insight. They like to smile and wink and provoke a wry nod of the head. They're inclined to push at the edges of experience—inviting us to look again, listen again, consider again just who and how they are.

So what would happen if we followed these Characters into the future? How would their present revelations deepen or change? How would what seemed oblique at a first encounter become obvious—and vice versa? In my life—in yours—will Anger ever be a real friend? Could Blame, so attuned to others, ever evolve into Praise? Once Delight moves into the house, is there danger of transformation into Tedium? Dependence and Truth, Leisure and Wonder, Grief and Mundane, Mystery and Silence—what will become of these partners and their partnerships? Is there any hope, any relief or redemption for Rage or Revenge? Will Integrity and his teammates win medals, or will their wrestling prowess go unremarked—and how will they deal with defeat? What effect will her sense of excitement about "that day" have on Routine? Will Vulnerability, so safe and tranquil in her garden, someday confide the pain behind her tears or the courage it takes to work the soil?

The answers to these questions are legion. They differ for each individual; they differ over time for the same individual. As with these questions, so with these Characters—and all their cousins. Their fascinating and frustrating complexity allows them to play true while sharing some traits today and others tomorrow, while revealing some secrets to me and others to you. And thus it is that befriending *The Characters Within* is ever a verb of progressive tense and active voice. As you listen and speak, as the conversation continues to unfold, may you be intrigued, amused, amazed, inspired by the cast of Characters within and beyond this book—that is, by those alluring and enduring Characters *you* harbor and with whom you spend your days . . . your nights . . . your life.

ALSO FROM ACTA PUBLICATIONS

The Legend of the Bells and Other Tales: Stories of the Human Spirit by John Shea
Master storyteller and theologian John Shea offers 25 of his favorite stories, drawn from a variety of sources, followed by a thought-provoking reflection on the spiritual meaning of the story. (181 pages, $12.95)

Everyday People, Everyday Grace: Daily Meditations for Busy Christians by George R. Szews
Short vignettes and insights into the presence of grace in the everyday lives of ordinary people are coupled with insightful and unexpected Scripture verses. (368 pages, $9.95)

Pray with All Your Senses: Discovering the Wholeness Jesus Brings by Lo-Ann and David Trembley
Exercises and activities that teach how to use all five human senses of sight, smell, taste and hearing—along with a heightened sense of self and movement—to experience God more fully. (128 pages, $8.95)

Home is a Holy Place: Reflections, Prayers and Meditations Inspired by the Ordinary
Author Mark Boyer uses over thirty everday household items like an apron, electricity, a robe, keys, and a zipper as the subjects of folksy yet profound reflections on discovering the spiritual in the ordinary. (88 pages, $6.95)

Daily Meditations (with Scripture) for Busy...Moms, Dads, Grandmas, Grandpas, Couples
This series of reflection books, each written by a different author, have proven to be a big hit. Each down-to-earth meditation is illuminated by a carefully chosen Bible quote that offers an insight into the spirituality of family life. (368 pages each, $8.95 each)

Available from religious book sellers or call 800-397-2282 in the U.S. or Canada.